HOW TO
MANIFEST

For Murphy and Hamish who
manifest the best day ever,
each morning.

Published in the United States by Ten Speed Press, an imprint of Random House,
a division of Penguin Random House LLC, New York.
TenSpeed.com
RandomHouseBooks.com

Ten Speed Press and the Ten Speed Press colophon are registered trademarks
of Penguin Random House LLC.

Originally published in paperback in Great Britain by Michael O'Mara Books
Limited, London.

Library of Congress Control Number: 2022942415

Hardcover ISBN: 978-1-9848-6196-2
eBook ISBN: 978-1-9848-6197-9

Printed in China

Acquiring editor: Kaitlin Ketchum | Project editors: Kimmy Tejasindhu and
Want Chyi | Production editor: Ashley Pierce
Design manager: Annie Marino | Production designer: Mari Gill
Production manager: Jane Chinn
Proofreader: Jennifer McClain
Publicist: Natalie Yera | Marketer: Brianne Sperber

10 9 8 7 6 5 4 3 2 1

First US Edition

HOW TO MANIFEST

Bring Your Goals into Alignment
with the Alchemy of
the Universe

GILL THACKRAY

TEN SPEED PRESS
California | New York

Contents

Introduction:
What Is Manifesting?

Nothing happens until something moves.
When something vibrates, the electrons
of the entire universe resonate with it.
Everything is connected.

ALBERT EINSTEIN

Manifesting isn't new. It has been practiced by ancient wisdom traditions around the world for thousands of years. When you manifest, you begin to invite the law of attraction into your life. You begin to acknowledge how the universe works—that each one of us has the potential to create our own reality.

In its simplest form, manifesting is the theory that we are able to work collaboratively with the universe by applying a series of principles to shape our world. By setting an intention to change our thoughts, feelings, and actions, we become the architect of our own lives. When you harness manifesting practices, you can build the conditions to transform your life and create the reality you truly desire.

We move toward what we focus on. When we manifest, we recognize how our beliefs about ourselves, the world, and what we deserve can dramatically change what we experience in life. Our mindset has a huge impact on how our life unfolds. If you have a fixed, negative mindset and you don't believe it's possible to change your life, that's pretty much what you'll experience. That's where your energy will flow. All you'll notice are obstacles, blocks, and limits. Manifesting is an opportunity to create a new way of looking at the world— to re-create.

A positive mindset is quite empowering. It creates a powerful vibration that attracts positive experiences. When you manifest, you bring your goals into alignment with the alchemy of the universe. When you step into a manifesting mindset, you're shedding your past and creating a new, beautiful reality. As you take action, the loving energy of the universe rises to meet you.

If you're stuck in negativity, you can change your story and your mindset. That's where the magic of manifesting comes in. You're dreaming a new reality into being. Don't believe me? You don't need to right now. Suspend your judgment and try these transformational practices anyway. You've got nothing to lose; think of it as a do-over to get back on track with any goals you haven't achieved and see what happens.

If I manifest my goals, am I bypassing a spiritual path? Will I miss valuable life lessons? No. Manifesting is your opportunity to achieve your potential and become an awesome force for change in the world. It is an incredibly powerful tool that you can use for the planet and everyone else on it. Manifesting

isn't about being self-centered or narcissistic. It's about reinvention and transformation. Becoming the driver instead of a passenger. You can use it selflessly to become a powerful cocreator for global change and to give your focus, time, and resources to others. Maybe you're passionate about strengthening your community, healing the environment, or initiating activism that creates a collective shift. Manifesting provides a practical pathway to meet the challenges that the planet faces. It can be world-changing. It's up to you how you use it.

Believe you can and
you're halfway there.

THEODORE ROOSEVELT

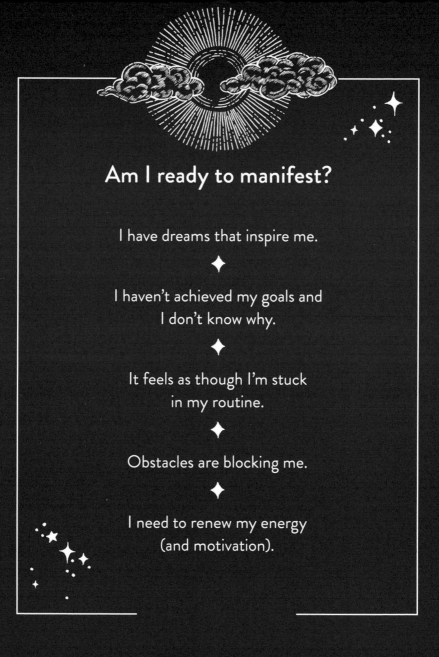

Am I ready to manifest?

I have dreams that inspire me.

✦

I haven't achieved my goals and
I don't know why.

✦

It feels as though I'm stuck
in my routine.

✦

Obstacles are blocking me.

✦

I need to renew my energy
(and motivation).

My limiting beliefs about who
I am and what I can do stop me
in my tracks.

✦

The people around me also have
limiting beliefs.

✦

I know there's power in me
somewhere, I just don't know
how to access it.

✦

I'm ready to change my mindset.

✦

I have a deep inner whisper telling
me it's time.

Manifesting is more than simply creating an image of what you want in your mind. Dreaming and creating a vision of the kind of life that you want is only part of the story. On its own, that won't change much. You need to be proactive and do something with that vision. That's where manifesting comes in. It's more than a vision; it's taking action and calling in the power of the universe. There are four key stages to manifesting.

Four-stage manifesting formula

Vision

+

Mindset

+

Intention

+

Action

= Manifestation of your goal

Once all of these components are in place, you'll notice a shift. When you manifest, you're calling in the universe to cocreate alongside you.

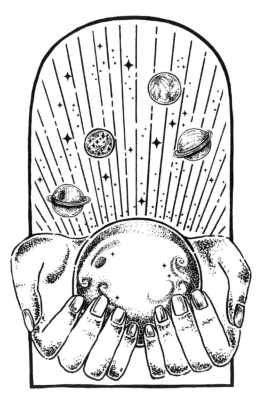

Creating a Vision

Light a candle and create a sacred space where you're able to really listen to your inner self. Reflect on where you are now and where you want to be. Think about the areas of your life that you want to change. Give yourself permission to dream big. Don't limit yourself or think about the "how" at this stage.

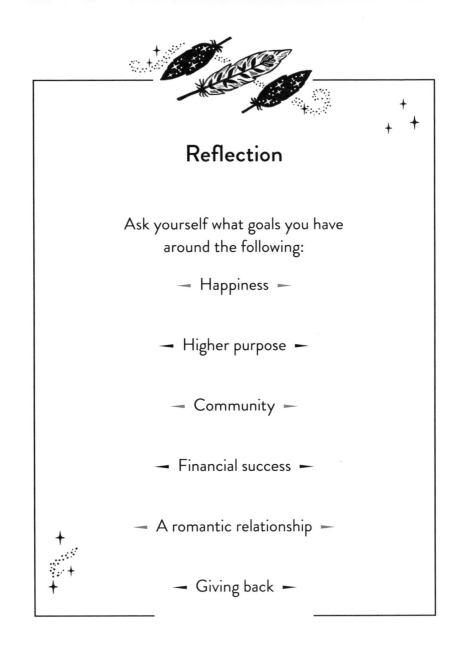

Reflection

Ask yourself what goals you have
around the following:

 — Happiness —

 — Higher purpose —

 — Community —

 — Financial success —

 — A romantic relationship —

 — Giving back —

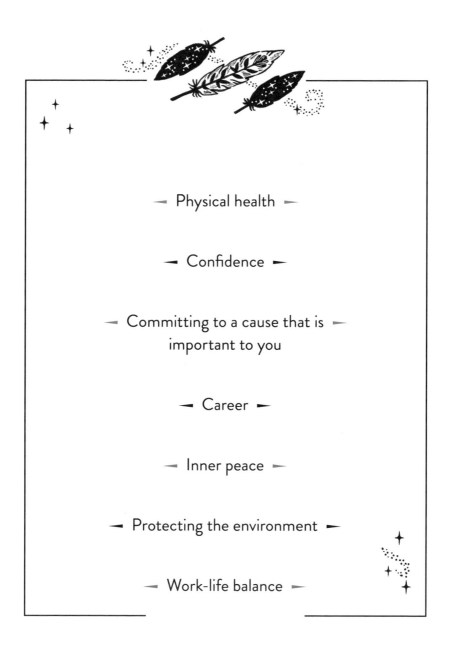

Physical health

Confidence

Committing to a cause that is
important to you

Career

Inner peace

Protecting the environment

Work-life balance

Exercise: Visualization

When you visualize what you want to embody, you begin to change your vibration, calling in the law of attraction. Think of it as a potent form of daydreaming that you can do daily. A way of bringing your brilliance into the manifest world. Consistent practice is key. It takes around sixty seconds to visualize each goal.

1. Find somewhere that you won't be disturbed. Take three deep breaths and relax your body.

2. Bring your goal to mind with clarity. Imagine it is happening, right here, right now. What does it look like? Intentionally create a kaleidoscopic palette of positive colors, textures, and background. What can you hear? Is there a tapestry of sound? Do you feel vital and energetic?

3. What do you feel? Elation? Pride? Excitement? Serenity? Contentment? Gratitude?

4. How do others treat you? What is the tempo of your life? Which subtle energies do you notice?

5. Take time to sense everything that you would feel, see, and hear if you had already achieved your goal. Immerse yourself in the magic of this new reality.

If visualization isn't for you,
create a vision board instead, see page 22.

Exercise: Vision board

For this you will need old magazines with images that inspire you, scissors, glue, and paper.

1. Make time to reflect. Light a candle and meditate upon your goals. This is a magical exercise where you can allow yourself to daydream without limits. Tune into the message from your soul.

2. Using old magazine images, create a collage of what you dream of achieving. Choose images that connect you emotionally and spiritually to your goal.

3. Once you've made your vision board, surrender to the universe and ask for assistance. Be receptive to whatever comes next.

4. Place your vision board somewhere prominent and devise a short daily ritual where you meditate on it every day.

Your Mindset Audit

Here's where you're going to explore any old stories, tired and worn-out mental habits, and limiting beliefs around your goals. We all have times when impostor syndrome hits us, and we're convinced we're not good enough or smart enough. You're not alone. There's nothing wrong with you. Everyone feels like this from time to time. It's how you respond to those thoughts that makes the difference. People who achieve their goals aren't made of different stuff. They've just learned some things about how to manage those feelings. This is where you begin to rewire your self-belief. Ask yourself the following questions.

What's my inner narrative like around this goal?

◆

What stories am I telling myself?

◆

Where am I holding myself back?

◆

What new stories can I dream into being?

◆

What calls for inner work am I hearing?

◆

How can I align my thoughts with my goal?

Exercise: Reframing thoughts with positive affirmations

Researchers at Queens University, Toronto, discovered that the average person has around 6,500 thoughts a day. That's a manifesting opportunity not to be wasted. Your brain doesn't know the difference between what's real and what's imagined; it just knows what you tell it. Your thoughts shape your world, so it's important to become aware of them.

Once you start tracking your thoughts and "stories" it can feel like your inner critic is on speed dial, but remember that framing can be positive or negative. When you frame thoughts consciously, they begin working for you instead of against you, unlocking your gifts. Here's how.

Awareness

Become curious about your thoughts. Start to monitor them every day (it takes practice). As soon as you "catch" a thought, examine it.

Clarity

Ask yourself, is this thought moving me toward my goal? (Not sure? The clue's in your language. Any thought that includes "I can't," "won't," "should," or "never" is going to limit you.) If the answer is no, how can I reframe it?

○○ ─ **Reframe** ─ ○○

Take your thought and frame it in the positive. Use the present tense as if you are already confident in your skills and abilities—without limitations. For example: "I'm not good enough to find a job that pays well" focuses on what you don't have. It emanates from a place of scarcity, and that's what keeps our energy stuck.

So, we're going to supercharge that statement and shift ourselves into a place of confidence, as if you've already achieved your goal. Use "I am" instead of "I will," "I want," or "I'd like to be." You're in the process of becoming in each and every moment. Use "I am": "I am highly skilled and worthy of a job that pays me all I want and more."

— ∘ ∘ **Feel it** ∘ ∘ —

Scan your body. What would it feel like somatically if you felt this was true? Embody that frequency. Immerse yourself. Step into it and feel it in every cell.

∘ ∘ — **Put that new thought out into the universe** — ∘ ∘

Say it out loud. You are the one person who can make this happen.

Setting an Intention

—◆—

Focusing on what you don't want leaves you stuck in your old mindset. Reframe your intention positively and your energy will follow your new focus.

Exercise: How to set your intention

For this you'll need a pen and paper.

1. Bring your goal to mind. Remember to stay flexible. Intentions involve surrendering to the universe. It's possible that the law of attraction will bring you something way beyond what you're dreaming of—you don't want to miss it by being too rigid.

2. Write your intention down. For example, "I am confident and assertive."

3. What will you need to do to get there? You might decide to take a class on assertiveness or read a book on building confidence.

4. Reflect on your intentions daily. This will help you to remain focused and to connect emotionally with the universal law of attraction on your sacred manifesting journey.

Mapping your intention with action

Get ready to embark on an incredible journey. It's now time to get proactive and collaborate with the universe. Trust that the universe has her arms around you, supporting you, co-creating by your side as you design a map to actualize your dream. Remember to stay flexible—who knows where the journey will take you. If your goal is big, break it down into smaller steps.

What is the one thing I can do today
that will support my intention?

What goals can I set that will make the
biggest difference to achieving this intention?

Who can help me? Who can I talk to?

What resources are available to me?

What's likely to get in the way or
derail me? How can I overcome this?

Which areas of my personal growth
do I need to focus on?

How can I build my personal resources
(social support, resilience, skills, and knowledge)?

How can I make these steps part
of my routine?

Make your goals SMART

Specific, **M**easurable, **A**chievable, **R**ealistic, and **T**ime-bound

For example, an intention of "I want to be fitter" isn't framed in the positive ("want" comes from a place of lack) and it isn't SMART. It's not specific and we can't measure it. An intention of "I am fit, healthy, and happy with my body" could be broken down into the following SMART action points:

I will eat five portions of fruit and
vegetables every day.

✦

I will commit to going meat-free
every Monday.

✦

I will work out for forty-five
minutes, three times a week, on
Monday, Wednesday, and Saturday.

✦

I will practice a visualization ritual
for three minutes every day to
step into an image of a fit, healthy,
happy body—and really embody
that state.

Write down your goals and finish with a prayer to the universe.

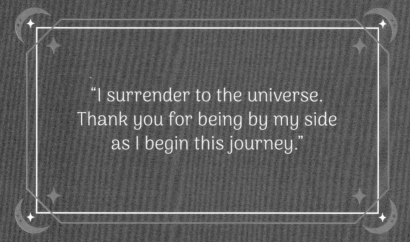

"I surrender to the universe.
Thank you for being by my side
as I begin this journey."

Remember that your goals are likely to radically change as things shift. As you transmute beliefs that have previously held you back (goodbye to those!), bigger and bolder dreams are going to emerge. In a year's time, you will barely recognize the person you were before, so it makes sense that you'll need to pivot and flex your ambitions accordingly.

It isn't what we say
or think that defines us,
but what we do.

JANE AUSTEN

Collaborating
with the Universe

Whatever you can do or dream
you can, begin it; boldness has genius,
power, and magic in it.

JOHANN WOLFGANG
VON GOETHE

Sometimes we're the ones holding ourselves back. We get in our own way, believing that we're not ready "yet." Waiting for the day when we feel good enough, clever enough, thin enough, or (fill in the blank) enough is a delay tactic. An urban myth. That day doesn't exist. We need to show up for ourselves to get from where we are now to where we want to go. Critical self-talk isn't in alignment with what you're manifesting. A fixed mindset will generate disharmony and keep you stuck.

When you hear that toxic self-talk:

Take three deep breaths.

Place both palms over your heart area.

Repeat after me: "I am enough."

Mystical transformation can only happen when you say YES to it, give it your consent. In order to cocreate with the beautiful, divine energy of the universe, we must take that first step. That means digging deep, pushing past those old feelings of not being good enough (they're not even true). Collaboration means tapping into your highest conscious potential, recognizing the extraordinary abundance that's there—and taking action. Begin your unique journey and watch as the forces of the universe conspire to help you manifest.

Developing a Manifesting Mindset

A positive mindset is open. It attracts opportunity and connections on the same positive level. A manifesting mindset recognizes that change doesn't happen instantaneously. As you begin your manifesting journey, it's important to remain open to whatever the universe sends you rather than sticking rigidly to your own preconceived ideas about what something looks like.

Your brain has a negativity bias. Our ancestors evolved that way to survive and avoid danger, but it can also work against us. Your brain is one of the most incredible tools that you have. You just need to know how to use it. Like any journey, there'll be ups and downs and curveballs. It takes time to rewire old thought patterns. You'll have days when you slip back into old, limited thinking. That's okay. During times like these, you'll need to recharge your energy field, renewing and maintaining your positive vibrations.

If you've ever set a goal and run out of bandwidth somewhere along the road to achieving it, you'll know how important energy is.

Exercise: Recharging your energy field

Remaining open to the flow of the exercise is crucial for manifesting. Grounding will help you to feel more centered, calm, and in control. It will also help you to develop a relationship with the creative energies of the universe, connecting you to your destiny.

Create a daily energy ritual where you ground yourself. Choose from the list below to get started.

Find a meditation space. You need to create quiet and calm. Listen for inner guidance, messages from the universe, and the next step on your destiny path.

✦

Journal. Build journaling into your day. Write down your thoughts, feelings, and inspirations.

Physically ground yourself. Stand up and imagine that you have roots spreading out from your feet, deep into the earth. Visualize your roots going deep down into the ground— past tree roots, rocks, and moist earth, all the way to the heart of Mother Earth. Stand and feel connected, held, and supported by that divine love.

✦

Connect with your environment. Walk in nature and eco-meditate by listening to the birds, the breeze, and the leaves rustling in the wind.

✦

Verbally ground yourself. Use a word or phrase as an anchor:

"I am loved,
I am a child of the universe."

The 369 Method

- ✦ -

This method is attributed to Serbian physicist and inventor Nikola Tesla, who believed that the numbers 3, 6, and 9 held a profound, universal significance. Patterns of 3, 6, and 9 occur in mathematics, art, nature, and throughout the universe. The 369 Method encourages you to revisit your goals throughout the day, reinforcing them and maintaining your focus. Remember that we move toward whatever it is that we focus on, and the 369 Method keeps your aspirations right at the forefront of your mind.

Write down your objective. For example, "I want a loving partner who shares and supports my goals." Do this three times in the morning, six times in the afternoon, and nine times at night. Repeat the method for forty-five days. Set an alarm to remind yourself until you've embedded the 369 Method into your day as a habit.

Tarot

— ✦ —

Many people feel uneasy about using Tarot cards. That's due to misunderstanding and myth. Tarot reading is an ancient mystical practice used across many cultures, dating all the way back to the fifteenth century. Think of the cards as a tool to focus your thinking, enabling you to tap into divine wisdom as you explore a particular goal or issue that you want to manifest.

Most Tarot cards are based on the popular Rider-Waite Tarot deck created in 1909, but today you'll find a host of beautifully illustrated decks depicting a variety of metaphors, symbols, and archetypes. The cards are split into two categories: twenty-two Major Arcana cards and fifty-six Minor Arcana cards. There are usually seventy-eight cards in a Tarot deck, while Oracle decks can have any number of cards. Choose a deck that you feel intuitively drawn to.

Exercise: One-card pull

If you're new to the cards, you can do a simple "one-card pull" to begin to familiarize yourself with them. You can use the cards for anything and everything that's coming up in your life, gaining insights around your personal development, relationships, and career, or simply where to place your focus for the month ahead. You decide.

1. Reflect on one of your manifesting goals and begin to tap into your inner wisdom. Ask an open question, for example, "What should I focus on with this goal?" Or, "What do I need to know about this goal?" You'll get better results if you avoid questions that only have yes or no answers. Write your question on a piece of paper and place it to one side.

2. Quiet your mind and phase out any negative self-talk around the issue. Let go of any preconceived ideas that you might have around your goal. Meditate on your question and shuffle the cards.

3. Traditionally, the deck is cut after shuffling. You can cut the deck and place the two halves together again or leave them in two separate piles.

4. Choose a card randomly. There's no need to try to orchestrate an answer. Connect with your intuition and inner wisdom to interpret the card. There are no right or wrong answers. Be still and listen to what presents itself.

5. When you see the card, what is your initial impression? If, for example, you draw The Magician, notice how you feel as you first see the image. Reflect on the detail you notice. Do you have a felt sense in your body around the card, such as a feeling of joy or peace or excitement?

It is never too late
to be what you might
have been.

GEORGE ELIOT

Exercise: The three-card spread

A spread is a pattern for laying out the cards that you draw. The way the cards are placed together creates a unique dynamic, connecting the cards and producing the reading. Each card represents a different angle or perspective regarding your question. There are many different layouts, but we're going to begin with a simple three-card spread.

1. Create a sacred space to work in. This means making sure you're in an environment that is tranquil and where you won't be disturbed.

Ground yourself in whatever way works for you, whether it's by meditating, relaxing, or listening to music. Bring yourself into neutral, dialing down your internal chatter to encourage a calm, impartial, receptive energy.

2. Bring your goal or issue to mind. Think of three interrelated questions around this issue. For example, if you're thinking about your career, then the questions could be:

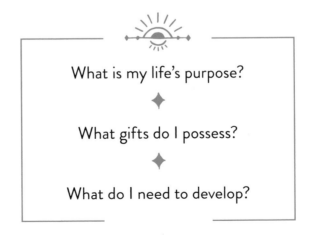

What is my life's purpose?

✦

What gifts do I possess?

✦

What do I need to develop?

3. Shuffle the deck and cut it. Randomly choose three cards and place them face down in a row.

Card one = What is my life's purpose?

✦

Card two = What gifts do I possess?

✦

Card three = What do I need to develop?

4. Turn over one card at a time. Ask yourself, What do I notice? How do I feel? What is my intuition telling me about this card in relation to my question? Use all of your senses to check in with yourself. If you're not familiar with the cards, you can check the card's meaning either online or using the book that most decks come with. Consider your three guiding questions as you interpret each card.

5. Make notes as you turn each card and research its meaning. Once you've worked with all three cards, you've got your very own three-card reading to help you on your manifesting journey.

Connecting with
Your Nature Ally

Ancient Celtic wisdom traditions viewed nature allies as spiritual guides in natural form, which protect and support you on your journey through life. They can present themselves in any natural form: plants, trees, stones, lakes, rivers, mountains, elements, or animals. Your nature ally is there to help you explore and develop your potential. It's a special relationship. Nature allies can reveal themselves in meditations, as a felt sense, in visions, dreams, or shamanic journeys.

The relationship with a nature ally is a healing one. Your ally connects you with your innate power and who you are becoming. Nature allies help throughout life, not just when you are manifesting. You'll find that they're incredible teachers, often revealing your shadow side or illuminating blocks that you need to work on in order to manifest your goals. Developing a relationship with your nature ally in manifestation will help you to step forward in your own power and reimagine your destiny.

Exercise: Journey to connect with your nature ally

Your nature ally may surprise you. Traditionally, you don't choose your nature ally; your nature ally chooses you. Let go of any preconceived notions of the ally you want to have and be prepared to be surprised.

1. Start a nature-ally journal and write down your intention to connect with your nature ally.

2. Find a safe, tranquil space where you won't be disturbed, either outside in nature or indoors.

3. Make yourself comfortable. Relax your body. Close your eyes, if that feels right for you.

4. Visualize a place in nature where you feel comfortable and safe. This is the place where you'll begin your journey. You see a sacred pathway; walk along it, feeling your feet connect with the earth. You come to a beautiful forest, smelling the scent of pine needles in the air. The trees are surrounded by serene mountains. You walk into a tranquil clearing.

5. Sit down on the grass and ask for your nature ally to come to you. Pay close attention to all of your senses. If a natural form approaches you, ask, "Are you my nature ally?" If the answer is no, it's okay. Continue to wait. If the answer is yes, ask it if it has any messages for you.

6. Once your conversation is over, return along the sacred pathway, bringing your nature ally with you. If no nature ally arrives, it's okay. Journey again on another day; remember it's a process that can take time—your nature ally may not be on your schedule.

7. Record your encounter and the details of your journey in your journal. You might notice that there are signs of your nature ally appearing in your life, so write these down too.

8. Develop a personal relationship with your nature ally by working with it on a regular basis to discover what it has to teach you.

The beginning is
always today.

MARY WOLLSTONECRAFT

Full-Moon Rituals

Grandmother moon supports your personal growth and creativity. Think of the full moon as an energetic powerhouse when it comes to manifesting. The full moon is an enormously powerful opportunity to connect with the universe and set new intentions. It's a time of releasing, cleansing, letting go, receiving, and giving thanks to that supreme Goddess energy. It's a time of empowerment.

Exercise: Full-moon fire ceremony

A fire ceremony is a sacred ritual. Performing this ceremony during a full moon can be a powerful way to release fear and negative self-talk and help you let go of what you no longer need. As well as purifying, it's a monthly manifesting opportunity to invite in new thoughts, feelings, and behaviors, and to call in deep and permanent transformation.

If you're able to hold your full-moon fire ceremony outdoors, under the gaze of the moon, you'll find it has an incredibly special dynamic. If you don't have access to an outside space, this ceremony can be done indoors using a candle.

What you'll need

Indoor ceremony: You'll need a candle, lighter, and wooden cocktail picks, coffee stirrers, or matchsticks.

Outdoor ceremony: You'll need a lighter, three sticks, and a metal container for your fire. A barbecue or aluminum takeout container works fine. Double-check that the space is safe for a fire and have a bucket of water at hand in case you need to put it out.

Set your intention for the ceremony

What do you want to let go of? Past hurts?
Self-doubt? The opinions of others? Anger?
Anything you want to say goodbye to or forgive?
Is there part of you that needs to heal?

"I release . . ."

✦

What would you like to invite in? Renewed
motivation for your goals? More momentum?
Inspiring insights? Meaningful connections?
Is there something that you want for your
community or the planet?

"I invite in . . ."

✦

What are you grateful for? Your successes? The
support that you've received from the universe?
Any lessons that you've learned?

"I'm grateful for . . ."

1. Feel the powerful, feminine energy of the moon: her intense, healing silver light illuminating you. Breathe in the cool night air. Relax. Open yourself up to any lessons that the moon has for you. Feel your awareness expanding.

2. With reverence, watch the fire flicker and glow. Connect with your ancestral energy as you watch the fire. Sit with it.

3. When you feel it's time, take one of your sticks. Place it between your hands, raise it to your lips, and blow into it the thing that you are grateful for. Now give it to the fire. Thank the universe for supporting your journey.

4. Now take another stick. Place it between your hands, raise it to your lips, and blow into it the thing that you want to release. Now give it to the fire.

5. Pick up your final stick. Place it between your hands, raise it to your lips, and blow into it the thing that you would like to invite into your life. Place your stick into the fire as an offering for Mother Earth.

6. If you are able to, it's traditional to remain with the fire until the flames die down to glowing embers. If you can't, use the water to extinguish the flames (or blow the candle out if you're indoors). Give thanks to the fire before you leave it.

Manifesting Through Chakras

— ✦ —

Your chakras are centers of energy in your body. Pronounced "cha-kruh," chakra means "spinning wheel" or "disc" in Sanskrit. There are eight main chakras in the center of your body, running from the base of your spine to the crown of your head. Each chakra opens at the front and back of the body. You can't see them or touch them, but you'll feel the difference when they're aligned. This is how your prana, or life force, runs freely through your body. Many cultures recognize that there are hundreds of chakras or energy meridians in the body—however, there are always the eight major chakras.

The eight major chakras

8. Soul chakra (Murdhanta). White. Your spiritual connection to the universe, the seat of the soul.

 7. Crown chakra (Sahasrara). White or Violet. Connected to spirituality and purpose.

 6. Third-eye chakra (Ajna). Indigo. Linked to intuition and instinct.

 5. Throat chakra (Visuddha). Blue. Linked to communication and your power to manifest.

 4. Heart chakra (Anahata). Green. Linked to love, compassion, forgiveness, and intimacy.

 3. Solar plexus chakra (Manipura). Yellow. Responsible for confidence, self-esteem, and safety.

 2. Sacral chakra (Svadhisthana). Orange. Linked to creativity, pleasure, and emotions.

 1. Root chakra (Muladhara). Red. Responsible for safety, trust, and groundedness.

Chakras can become unbalanced by stale or heavy prana (energy) from thoughts, life events, memories, or emotions. When this happens, it can leave chakras overactive or underactive, affecting your well-being. If there's stagnant energy in a chakra, you'll notice physical or emotional imbalance.

You can restore balance in your chakras with meditation, yoga, and visualization. When our chakras spin free and clear, our mind, body, and spirit are balanced. By understanding the chakras, you can work with these energy centers to keep them open and aligned, maintaining your energy flow. When they're clear, you'll notice that your energy, well-being, and inner narrative are optimized along with your ability to manifest.

Exercise: Chakra-balancing visualization

This meditation will activate your energetic potential by clearing and cleansing your chakras.

1. Stand with both feet flat on the floor. Exhale and imagine that there are silver roots emerging from your feet, going deep down into the earth. They wrap around tree roots, moving past rocks as they go deeper and deeper into the earth, grounding you.

2. Imagine a beautiful white flower about five fingers above the crown of your head. Visualize the petals opening into a beautiful lotus. This is your soul chakra, creating a bridge between you and the universe.

3. Bring your attention to the crown of your head. Conjure an image of a thousand-petalled white or violet flower. This is your crown chakra. Watch as the flower blooms until each petal has outstretched.

4. Now move your focus to the forehead. See an indigo flower here, opening up its petals. This is your third-eye chakra.

5. Next, bring your attention to your throat. Visualize a bright blue, turquoise flower opening: this is your throat chakra.

6. As you move further down, you see a green flower beginning to unfurl in your heart area. This is your heart chakra.

7. Now move to your solar plexus. You notice a yellow flower's petals unfolding. This is your solar plexus chakra.

8. Next, as your attention is drawn to just below your navel, you see an orange flower opening, your sacral chakra.

9. Finally, you move to the base of your spine, observing a red flower opening. This is your root chakra.

10. Return to the white lotus right at the top, your eighth chakra. Imagine there is a pure, radiant, white healing light streaming all the way down from the universe. Breathe in as you feel the light flow down, through the white lotus, down into your crown chakra.

11. Follow the light as it illuminates each chakra, one by one: your third-eye chakra, throat, heart, solar plexus, sacral, and root chakras. You feel it gently moving down into each chakra, circulating, entering every cell of your body with its healing energy. The light expands and begins to pool in each chakra until it is overflowing.

12. As the light meets pockets of stale energy, it gently permeates them, dissolving and washing away anything that you no longer need, anything that no longer serves you.

The Wheel
of the Year

The Celtic wheel of the year, wheel of life, or sacred calendar is an ancient symbol observing the seasons of the year. Honored by many cultures, it comes in various forms, representing health, balance, and spiritual healing on your soul's journey through life. This metaphysical circle is continuous, and you may choose to walk it many times to connect to your potential.

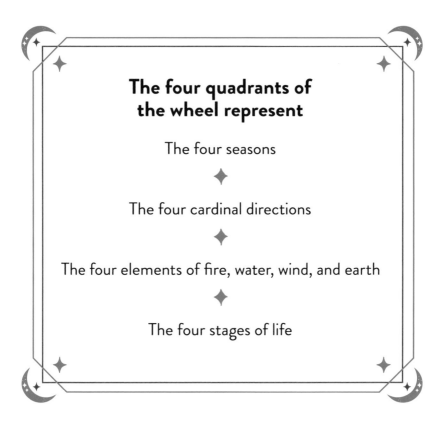

The four quadrants of the wheel represent

The four seasons

✦

The four cardinal directions

✦

The four elements of fire, water, wind, and earth

✦

The four stages of life

The wheel connects us to the earth, elements, seasons, and the divine universe, teaching us as we walk through each direction. Amplifying our intentions, it symbolizes the circle of life and the four parts of ourselves: spiritual, emotional, psychological, and physical. All of these personal aspects need to be in balance when we manifest.

Exercise: Building your wheel of the year

Think of the wheel as a map, an experiential wisdom path toward your authentic self. This exercise has three purposes:

To create a sacred space that connects you to the universe.

✦

To help you understand yourself, your motivations, strengths, areas for development, and purpose as you work through it.

✦

To provide a physical space where you can go to connect with your divine wisdom.

Gather some stones to mark out your circle. Make it big enough to sit or walk in. Use a compass or app to work out where north, south, west, and east are. These are known as the cardinal directions. Create a section for each of the four directions. Center yourself and align with nature.

North/winter = inner landscape
A time for regeneration, planning, setting
new intentions and goals

East/spring = sowing
New beginnings. Nurturing and nourishing yourself

South/summer = time of abundance and light
Gratitude for positive changes and letting
go of what's no longer needed

West/autumn = rest and renewal
Gratitude for walking your soul journey

Step into the North/winter direction

Connect with the reflective North energy. What can the North teach you about your inner landscape? What changes do you want to work on internally? What no longer serves you as you manifest? What new intentions and goals will you bring to life in this time of regeneration and creativity? This is time to begin planning.

Take a moment to connect with the spring energy of the East

Are there any messages for you here? In this direction, you're planting practical seeds that will help maintain manifesting momentum. How can you nourish and nurture yourself? Do you want to make changes to your diet, step up your exercise routine, or create more downtime so that you can recharge? This could include spending time in nature and connecting with Mother Earth, or perhaps praying and chanting in ceremony or ritual. You might even decide to plant some love in the soil of the universe by volunteering, practicing random acts of kindness, or doing something for the environment. Giving something back is part of universal balance, reciprocity. What goes around, comes around.

When you've completed the East, sit or stand in the South/summer direction

Connect with the abundant energy here; does it have a message for you? Ask yourself, what have I achieved? How can I remain connected to my soul's journey? Are there emotional patterns I want to let go of? Blocks I want to release and push through? Developing clear boundaries, living consciously, and speaking your truth might be an important aspect to develop in this direction.

Move toward the autumnal energy of the West

How does it feel in the West? Reflect on rest and renewal, how you can maintain your emotional equilibrium. For example, creating a strategy for when things don't go to plan. Learning more about resilience and mindset is another way to honor your sacred journey and remain on track.

Working with the elements of the wheel

The elements offer an opportunity to explore the wheel in tandem with your inner journey. You may walk this path many times, there is no beginning or end. It's a lifelong journey, an endless cycle. Each time you journey you'll learn something new about yourself, the world, and the spirit of the universe, which sits in the center of the wheel.

― Earth (North) ―

This element governs abundance, grounding, and wisdom. Reflect on how you ground yourself. Who and what do you connect to? Do they support your goals? Are you surrounded with solid, fertile sustenance? Do you provide the same to others? As you grow, acknowledge your internal wisdom, stepping into your personal power.

― Air (East) ―

This is the cognitive arena. Connect deeply to this life-giving element. Do you have clarity around your goals? Does your outer world reflect your inner world? Do your thoughts, words, and actions mirror the energy that you want to create?

― Fire (South) ―

Relating to transformation, spirituality, and passion. As you walk this ancient, universal mandala, connect to the cosmos. What evokes passion in you? What is your life's purpose? How can you nurture it, feeding the flame? If you want to purify and shed old habits, offer them to fire with thanks as you transform, beginning to burn brightly in the world.

― Water (West) ―

The sphere of emotions, intuition, and compassion. Water the seeds of your future goals by becoming sensitive to your emotions. Without judgment, notice the information they contain. Create space for silence, regularly attending to the whisper of your intuition. What does it tell you? Are you in flow or could you benefit from revisiting your goals as you are becoming?

Thank the universe before you leave your wheel. Visit the elements whenever you need to recharge or reflect on something new in your manifesting journey.

Cultivating Gratitude

Acknowledging what you already have as you go on your journey is crucial to manifesting. Research has shown that, as well as supercharging your well-being, daily gratitude will also keep you in a positive mindset. Even if reaching your goals isn't happening overnight (and it probably won't be), it's important to thank the universe daily for every single step forward.

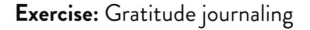

Exercise: Gratitude journaling

Researchers at Penn State University have found that keeping a daily gratitude journal improves your well-being and optimism, two attributes that are key on your manifesting journey. Here's how to cultivate more gratitude.

Create a gratitude journal. Make, and honor,
a commitment to write in it every day.

✦

Your gratitude journal is unique to you and
charts your personal journey. Make it your own.
At the end of each day, write down three things
that you are grateful for. They can be big ("I
got that promotion!") or small things ("The sun
shone today").

✦

Be specific. Focus on the people, acts of
kindness, and thoughtfulness that happened
throughout your day. As you write, bring those
moments to life and really savor them.

✦

On the days you feel low, and are struggling,
writing in your journal is even more important.

Manifesting Mindfully

— ✦ —

As you manifest, you'll need to remain focused. Profound transformation is going to require your attention. Mindfulness helps us to be in the present moment, remaining aware of what's happening as it happens. The more mindful you are, the more you'll begin to notice what requires your attention, subtle changes, and chance encounters.

You can also use mindfulness to monitor your self-talk, becoming kinder, more compassionate, and less judgmental when things don't go as you'd planned. It can be easy to get lost in negative thinking when that happens, reinforcing feelings of unworthiness and lack. We're often socialized to believe that we're not enough. When we fail, it just confirms that we're not smart enough, thin enough, capable enough, or whatever it is that we feel we lack, and down the rabbit hole of beating ourselves we go.

This meditation will get you back on track when those insecurities rise to the surface. You are enough, just as you are. And failure? Well, that's just information that you're going to use on your journey.

Exercise: Mindful self-love meditation

You might be tempted to skip this meditation—sometimes people back away from the concept of self-love. Maybe the mere mention of it leaves you feeling uncomfortable and a bit icky, or you just don't want to turn into a narcissist. Most of us have the opposite problem. We simply don't love ourselves enough. Think of it this way: you can't pour from an empty cup. What you don't have, you can't give. Learning to love yourself, heal old wounds, and accept all parts of yourself is a radical act that can only bring more love and healing into the world. When you add self-love into the manifesting mix, you're reclaiming your natural state.

1. Relax. Close your eyes, if that feels comfortable. Bring your focus to your breath, slowing each in-breath and out-breath down gradually. Feel the rise and fall of your abdomen.

2. Plant the seeds for a landscape of inner calm. Place your hand on your heart area. Feel the warmth and support from your hand radiate outward. Notice the soothing, nurturing feeling of that warmth.

3. Sit and bring your awareness to what you need in this moment. Connect with the powerful energy and love of the universe. Offer yourself the blessings of gratitude, love, and forgiveness. As you exhale, say to yourself:

— I am enough. —

— When things don't go as planned, —
I use it as an opportunity.

— I believe in myself and my ability. —

— I am grateful for the lessons that —
have brought me here.

— I am confident. —

— I am worthy. —

— I choose positive thoughts. —

— I trust my intuition. —

— I attract good things into my life. —

— I let go of self-judgment and comparisons. —

— I am loving and kind to myself. —

— I am creating my own destiny. —
Every. Single. Day.

Crystals for Manifesting

—✦—

Crystals are believed to possess metaphysical healing properties and protective powers. Each crystal has its own vibrational energy. They can be used to cleanse heavy energy, protect, heal, and promote positivity. They can also be used to heal and support the chakras. If you've set an intention to manifest in a particular area of your life—for example, attracting a new relationship—creating a crystal grid or holding a crystal in your meditation practice can amplify your intention.

Before you buy crystals, ground yourself. Take a few deep breaths and set an intention to find the right one for whatever you want to manifest. You may find that you're drawn to a particular crystal, one that speaks to you. Pay attention to that intuition; these are the stones that you are being called to work with.

There are a few simple steps you'll need to follow before your crystals are ready to work with.

Cleanse

Crystals pick up vibrations and you'll want to clear any previous imprints before you begin. Traditionally, the smoke of burning sage or sticks of palo santo (Spanish for "holy wood") is used for cleansing. Known as "smudging," the popularization of this practice has become controversial. There are ethical concerns about using practices that are not part of your own ancestral tradition without the permission of the culture that they belong to. Overharvesting and ecological issues around sustainability can also make using them environmentally problematic. As an alternative, and to remain in the spirit of reciprocity or balance with the universe, I'd invite you to explore smoke-cleansing your crystal by using herbs native to your geographical area: for example, bay leaves, locally sourced wood, incense, or lavender. Another alternative is leaving your crystal in direct sunlight for twenty-four hours, or cleansing it by holding it briefly under running water.

Permission

Ask your crystal, "Do I have permission to work with you?" Wait. If you get a sense of calm, it's ready to work with you. If there's no sense of peace, choose a different crystal.

○ ○ ⟶ **Charge** ⟵ ○ ○

Place your crystal on a windowsill under a full moon to charge it with energy.

— ○ ○ **Program** ○ ○ —

This is where you focus your energy. Ground yourself and bring the issue you're manifesting to mind. Set an intention for the crystal. Maybe you want to be more grounded, so you could choose a stone aligned with that goal, such as carnelian, and program it with that intention. Think of this stage as uploading your manifestation into the crystal. If you want to heal emotional wounds, rose quartz would be a great crystal to work with to manifest that intention. Hold your crystal in your hand and bring your intention to mind, visualizing it, feeling it, sensing it with your whole body.

○ ○ — **Act** — ○ ○

Remember, you're cocreating with the universe. Take action in alignment with the intention that you have programmed into your crystal. If you chose a crystal piece of jewelery, wear it, sleep with it, or pop it in your pocket as you get to work on your goals.

Crystal properties

⤙ Rose quartz ⤚

Aligned with the heart chakra, rose quartz promotes love, relationships, and compassion. This is great for healing emotional wounds and clearing heavy energy so that you are creating a receptive state for your goal.

– Turquoise –

Considered sacred by Native American, Aztec, and Inca cultures, turquoise cultivates inner calm and protects against heavy energy, clearing any emotional fog. It is connected to the throat chakra, and will enable you to find your power, speak your truth, increase your presence, and manifest.

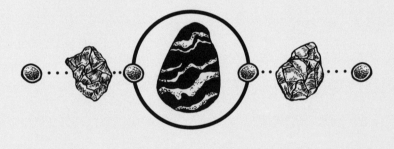

– Carnelian –

Synonymous with healthy self-esteem, courage, and overcoming envy, carnelian is often used to attract abundance and success. Linked to the sacral chakra, this stone is used for grounding and stability.

— Clear quartz —

This crystal has traditionally been used by shamanic cultures for healing and to dispel negative energy. This is the stone of focus and clarity and of sweeping away mental clutter. Closely associated with the crown chakra, it accelerates manifestation. The energy of clear quartz will assist you in aligning your goals with your highest potential, expanding your consciousness.

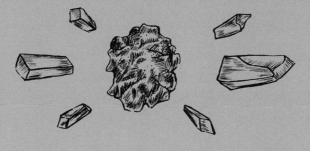

— Amethyst —

This crystal is known for enhancing inner wisdom and connection to your divine self. It soothes, bringing calm, balance, peace, and protection against psychic attack. Related to the crown and third-eye chakras, this is the stone of spirituality.

⤙ Smoky quartz ⤚

Once sacred to the Druids, this transformational stone promotes positivity, transmuting negativity and dispersing anxiety. Connected with the root chakra, it will balance your life-force energy, creating space for meaningful change. Smoky quartz will connect you to Mother Nature, relax you, and inspire you into action.

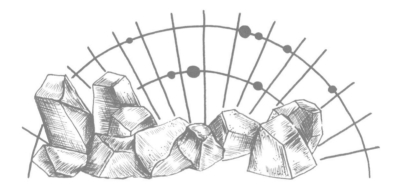

⤙ Hematite ⤚

Linked to the root chakra, hematite will ground and balance you, absorbing negative energy if you feel anxious or doubt your ability to manifest.

Exercise: Crystal-ring ritual

Based on the ancient wisdom of sacred geometry, this simple personal ritual will call on the synchronicity of the universe to help you manifest. Create a ring to channel the energy of your crystals and magnify your personal power.

You can construct your crystal ring indoors or, if you have space outside, in a garden or on a windowsill. You can arrange

crystals in a variety of shapes: grids, triangles, circles, or squares. For this exercise, you're going to arrange your crystals in a ring.

1. Ground yourself. Bring your goal to mind. Choose seven crystals that you feel drawn to work with.

2. Slow your breathing down and relax your body. Imagine the energetic membrane between you and the crystal dissolving.

3. Taking each crystal in turn, hold it in your right hand. Visualize the issue that you are manifesting. For example, if you want to attract a healthy, happy relationship, take rose quartz, hold it in your hand, and visualize love moving toward you, flowing through your arm and into your body. Imagine that love entering every cell of your body and flowing through your meridians (the channels and networks that energy, or life force, courses through).

4. Chanting has been practiced by ancient spiritual traditions for centuries. When you chant, you enter a meditative state, creating a unique energy. Chanting is a powerful way to send your intention out into the universe as you mindfully construct your ring.

5. Create a chant for your visualization. For rose quartz, you might chant

"I am loved."

6. Once you've finished your visualization, place your crystal in the ring on one of the seven points. Repeat with all your crystals until you have made a ring.

7. Take a moment to sit with your crystal ring, savoring the positive emotions and energy.

Incorporating crystals into your daily routine

Place your crystal ring somewhere you're able to see it daily. Spend a moment each day activating your connection with each crystal in your ring, bringing to mind your

vision + mindset + intention + action.

Remember, you'll move toward what you focus on. This is a great way to develop a transformational mindset.

Creating
Energetic Boundaries

—+—

When you begin to manifest, you change your own energy, and you'll find that you begin to attract all kinds of help and assistance from a range of people. The universe will create chance encounters and synchronicity that you just couldn't have imagined on your own.

Let's be realistic, though. Sometimes on your journey you'll bump into naysayers who'll tell you that your dreams are unachievable. Our culture can lionize cynicism. Sidestepping these energy vampires can be less than easy. They'll trigger your inner critic and cast doubt on your innate ability to manifest. That's okay: They don't know you or what you're capable of. It's really about them, their own limited worldview, and their own fear of failure (or success)—not yours.

You don't need to be a slave to someone else's opinion of you. You can deflect any uninvited negative energy or curveballs that come your way by creating energetic boundaries. These boundaries will help you to remain undeterred on your path, regardless of what comes at you.

Exercise: Create a daily grounding ritual

Choose from the following rituals to get started:

Meditate, walk, sit in nature, sleep well, be still

Guard your physical and emotional health by incorporating self-care into your routine.

Choose a crystal

Choose one that transmutes heavy energy, for example, smoky quartz, turquoise, or obsidian. Carry it with you or buy a ring or pendant with that crystal and let it do the work of wicking away any heavy energy that comes your way.

Limit your time around people who you know deplete your energy

If that doesn't work, you may decide on an energetic clear-out. Listen to the compass of your heart. Is it necessary to say goodbye to the people you've outgrown as your manifesting journey progresses? Wish them love and light and move on.

Say no

Give yourself permission to refuse anything and anyone that isn't in alignment with your manifesting goals (and your spirit).

Set reminders

Build time into your day to remind yourself of your goals (set an alarm and do practice the 369 Method).

Create review milestones

The full-moon ritual is a powerful opportunity to look back over the past few weeks, review what's working, revise what might not be, and introduce new goals. This will propel you toward the destiny that you are creating by manifesting.

Place a small bag of salt near your door

Salt has been used for centuries to protect and absorb heavy energies.

When you need guidance, go to your wheel of the year and connect with your higher power

If you find yourself in a stressful situation but you're nowhere near your wheel of the year, ground yourself in the four directions from exactly where you are. Draw the wheel on a piece of paper, adding the directions. In each direction, ask yourself, "What do I need in this moment?"

Seek greater connection with like-minded others

Check in with a soul tribe of people who support your goals. Reach out to these cheerleaders when you need them.

You have reached the end of this book and increased your capacity to manifest, but your journey is just beginning. The real work is in the transformation of yourself and the world around you. Forget doubt, self-censorship, and watching from the sidelines. Manifesting takes courage. If you see something that needs changing, or you want to be part of the solution for the world's problems, now is the time to tap into the magical well of your inner artist. You truly can create a shift in consciousness. Step in to the space of your fullest potential and reimagine your world. Align your goals with your heart, your soul, and your highest self and look forward to manifesting magnificent changes.

Twenty years from now you will be more disappointed by the things that you didn't do than by the ones you did do.

Explore, Dream, Discover.

MARK TWAIN